Scho

English

Key Stage 1

Revision Guide

Carol Matchett

Welcome to this book

What this book is for

This book will help you revise your reading and writing at the end of Year 2. It will help you check that you have understood the things you have learned in Key Stage 1.

What you need

- Paper, a pencil, crayons and an eraser.
- An adult to check your answers to the **Test yourself!** questions (or you can check them yourself).

How the book is set out

- There are pages about different reading and writing topics. These pages will remind you of what you have already learned at school.
- Look at the **contents** page (opposite) to see a list of all the topics in the book.
- You can start at the beginning and work through the book. Or you can choose your topics from the contents page.

How to work through a page

- Read the page carefully. Think about the examples. They will help you to understand.
- Some of the words are in orange. The Glossary on pages 62 and 63 tells you what they mean. Try to remember the orange words and their meanings.
- There is a **Remember** box on most pages. The **Remember** box lists one important thing that you need to know.
  Read it. Then cover it. What did it say? Can you remember?
- Most pages have **Test yourself!** questions. Read these questions. Then write your answers on a piece of paper.
  Ask an adult to check them against the right answers (pages 55 to 59), or you could check them yourself.
- Sometimes there is more than one 'right' answer and the answer page gives one example. If you are not sure about your answer, ask an adult to check it for you.
- Did you get a question wrong? Read the page again, more slowly. Then have another go.
- Are your answers right? Are you sure you understood everything? Yes? Then tick the circle in the corner of the page. Well done! Now you can move on to the next page.

Contents

page numbers

Reading skills
Reading for meaning 4
Reading difficult words 5
Blending phonemes 6
Blending more phonemes 7

Reading stories
Reading a story 8
The story 'Fair shares' 9
Checking your understanding 10
Explaining why 11
What do you think? 12
Thinking about characters 13

Reading non-fiction
Reading a non-fiction text 14
Features of non-fiction texts 15
Finding answers 16
Information in pictures 17
Information text 'The great recycle' 18
Thinking about the facts 19

Reading poetry
Reading a poem 20
Thinking about a poem 21

Making sentences
Writing in sentences 22
Linking ideas together 23
More linking words 24
Interesting sentences 25
Colourful sentences 26

Writing non-fiction
Types of non-fiction writing 27
Stop, think and organise! 28
Adding detail 29
How does it sound? 30
The right word 31

page numbers

Writing a letter 32
Writing a recount 33
Writing a postcard and writing a diary 34
Writing a report 35
Writing instructions 36

Writing stories
Thinking of ideas 37
Planning the story 38
Using time links 39
The details of the story 40
Finding the best word 41
Checking your writing 42

Writing a poem 43

Punctuation
Full stops and capital letters 44
Question marks and exclamation marks 45
Commas and speech marks 46

Spelling
Breaking words down 47
Words with long vowel sounds 48
Using syllables to help with spelling 49
More than one? 50
Word endings 'ing' and 'ed' 51
Learning to spell tricky words 52
Checking what you have learned 53

Handwriting 54

Answers 55, 56, 57, 58, 59
Curriculum chart 60, 61
Glossary 62, 63
Index 64

Note for teachers and parents

The Schofield & Sims Revision Guides are written by teachers, for use at school and at home. The Guides enable children to revise independently the work covered during the relevant key stage and, where appropriate, to prepare for the national tests (SATs). The focus is on clear explanations of the topics covered by the curriculum, all of which will already have been taught in school. Each English topic in this book is matched to the renewed Primary Framework for literacy (see the Curriculum chart on pages 60 and 61). For details of the other Revision Guides available, please see the back cover.

Reading for meaning

Reading is about making sense of the words on a page. Here are two useful things to remember when you are reading.

Always read aloud in your head

'Listen' to what you are reading so you can hear the meaning.

Check that what you are reading makes sense

If it makes sense you have probably read the **text** correctly.

If it does not make sense, you should:

- **stop** reading
- **go back** to the start of the **sentence**
- **read it again**. Look again at the words that did not make sense. See if you can work them out.

Test yourself!

Read these sentences aloud in your head. Underline the word that does not make sense.

1 "Hello, like girl," said the big bad wolf.

2 The frog helped off into the pond.

3 We all went on a trap to the zoo.

Remember

Always **read aloud in your head**. If something does not make sense, **stop, go back** and **read it again**.

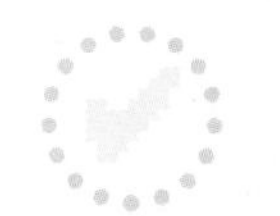

Reading difficult words

Look for clues

When you are reading, you might sometimes find a word that you do not know. Be a 'word detective'. Look for clues to help you work out the word.

Clue 1: Think about the rest of the sentence

If you follow this clue, you might think of a word that could fit. For example, think what word might fit the gap in this sentence:

Goldilocks sat down on the s_______ chair.

Clue 2: Look at the word

You might know part of the word. Then you can build the rest of the word from the bit you know.
For example:

small and **'est'** makes **smallest**

Clue 3: Look at the letters in the word

Say the sounds to go with the letters. Try **blending** the sounds together so you can hear the word.
For example:

c/r/ea/k makes **creak**

Clue 4: Break it up

If the word is long, break it into smaller parts. Each small part is called a **syllable**. Find each syllable and then put the word together. For example:

sud/den/ly makes **suddenly**

Remember

Look for **clues** to help you work out **difficult words**.

Go back and check

When you think you know the word, go back to the start of the sentence or paragraph. Read it again. Check that the word makes sense.

Goldilocks sat down on the **smallest** chair. **Creak! Suddenly** the chair broke!

Blending phonemes

You can read lots of words by saying their letter sounds (**phonemes**) and **blending** them together.

Sometimes two or three letters make one sound, as in:

c-r-a-sh b-ow-l ch-air

You need to know all the phonemes to read words.
Make sure you know the phonemes on these two pages.

Consonant phonemes

Consonant phonemes are sounds made by one or more consonants. For example:

1 a) 'ch' as in 'chips'

b) 'sh' as in 'shed'

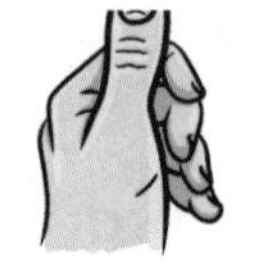

c) 'th' as in 'thumb'

d) 'ck' as in 'tick'

Long vowel phonemes

Many long **vowel** phonemes are made up of two or three letters. For example:

1 a) 'ee' as in 'bee'

b) 'ea' as in 'ice cream'

c) 'e-e' as in 'these'

2 a) 'ai' as in 'snail'

b) 'ay' as in 'tray'

c) 'a-e' as in 'plate'

3 a) 'ie' as in 'pie'

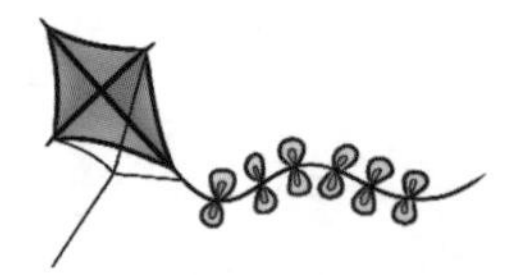

b) 'i-e' as in 'kite'

c) 'igh' as in 'light'

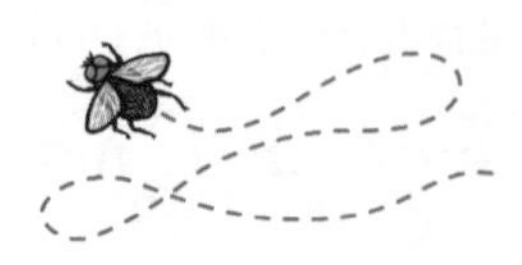

d) 'y' as in 'fly'

4 a) 'oa' as in 'boat'

b) 'ow' as in 'snow'

c) 'o-e' as in 'bone'

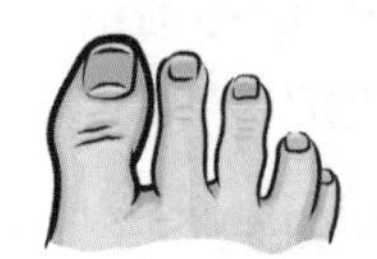

d) 'oe' as in 'toe'

Blending more phonemes

5 a) 'oo' as in 'spoon'

b) 'ue' as in 'blue'

c) 'u-e' as in 'cube'

d) 'ew' as in 'stew'

6 a) 'or' as in 'fork'

b) 'oor' as in 'door'

c) 'aw' as in 'paw'

d) 'ore' as in 'score'

7 a) 'ir' as in 'bird'

b) 'ur' as in 'burst'

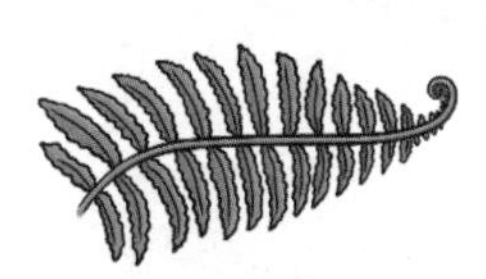

c) 'er' as in 'fern'

d) 'ear' as in 'Earth'

8 a) 'oy' as in 'toy'

b) 'oi' as in 'coin'

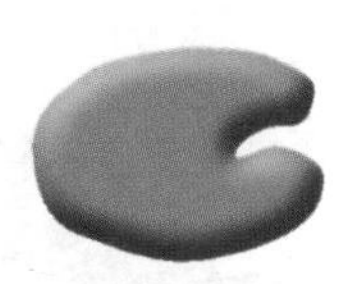

9 a) 'ow' as in 'brown'

b) 'ou' as in 'spout'

10 a) 'ar' as in 'car'

11 a) 'air' as in 'chair'

b) 'ear' as in 'bear'

c) 'are' as in 'square'

12 a) 'ear' as in 'tear'

b) 'eer' as in 'deer'

c) 'ere' as in 'sphere'

Test yourself!

Look again at all the phonemes opposite and above. Find **one other word** with each of these phonemes in it.

Remember

You can read lots of words if you know the **phonemes** (letter sounds).

Reading a story

When you read a **story**, always try to picture the **events** as you read about them. Imagine that you are watching the events like a film.

Here are some ideas that will help you to enjoy your reading.

Picture the main events

As you read, picture exactly what happens in the story. Think about each **character**. Think about where the story takes place and how and when the events happen.

Stop, think and remember

Stop reading sometimes, and see if you can remember everything that has happened in the story so far. Think about the events in the right order. Imagine yourself telling the story to someone else.

Think ahead

Decide what you think might happen next. Then read on to see if you were right.

Test yourself!

Read the story on page 9. As you read, picture in your head the events in the story.

Remember

When you read a story, read it aloud in your head. **Picture the events** as you read about them.

Reading a story

Follow the hints given on page 8 as you read and enjoy the story below.

Fair shares

There were once two bears called Oscar and Bruno. They were brothers but were very different.

One spring morning the two bears went fishing. Oscar liked fish, but he did not like fishing. He was lazy. He wanted his brother to do the hard work.

But brother Bruno was clever. He knew a way to trick Oscar into working.

"Let us share the work," Bruno said. "I'll do the fishing. You can get tired for me."
Get tired! Oscar did not like that idea very much.
"No way!" Oscar said. "I'll do the fishing. You can get tired for me."
"As you wish," Bruno smiled.

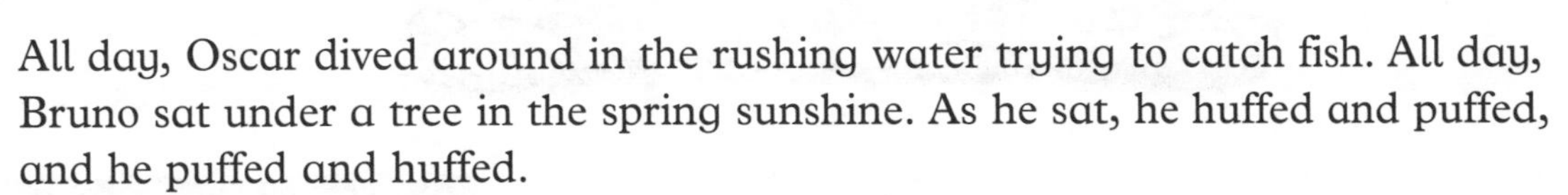

All day, Oscar dived around in the rushing water trying to catch fish. All day, Bruno sat under a tree in the spring sunshine. As he sat, he huffed and puffed, and he puffed and huffed.

"What hard work," Bruno said in a weary voice. "I am so tired!"

By the end of the day, Oscar had caught three fish.
"It is hard to share three fish," Bruno said. "You take them. I'll have the fish we catch tomorrow. We might get four or five tomorrow ..."

Four or five fish! Oscar liked the thought of that. He would let his brother Bruno take the three fish caught today. He would have tomorrow's catch.

So off went Bruno with the three fish. While Oscar had none.

But when the next day came, Bruno did not want to go fishing. He was too busy eating fish! And Oscar was too tired to go alone.

Checking your understanding

It is a good idea to think about a story you have just read. This will help make sure that you understand it. When you read a story as part of your school work, you may sometimes find questions at the end of it. The questions might begin with some of these words:

When ... ?   What ... ?   Where ...?   Who ... ?

Your answers to these questions will show how well you followed the story.

Here are some questions about the story 'Fair shares'.

1 When did the two bears go fishing?
2 What did Oscar do all day?
3 Where did Bruno sit all day?
4 Who went off with no fish at the end of the day?
5 What did Bruno do the next day?

This is the way to answer questions like these.

- Read the question carefully.
- Think about which part of the story the question is asking about.
- Go back and find that part of the story.
- Read the part again to find the words that give the answer.
- Write the answer down.

Test yourself!

Answer the questions on this page about the story 'Fair shares'. For each question, go back and underline the part of the story that tells you the answer.

Remember

Go back and **find the answer in the story**. Do not guess or just look at the pictures.

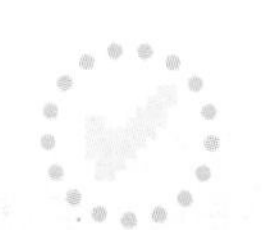

Explaining why

Some questions begin with the word 'Why'. Why questions check how well you understood important parts of the story.

Here are some why questions about the story 'Fair shares':

1. Why did Bruno smile when he said: "As you wish"?
2. Why did Bruno huff and puff as he sat under the tree?
3. Why did Oscar let Bruno have the three fish?
4. Why was Oscar too tired to go fishing the next day?

How to answer a why question

Explain or give reasons

Why questions need you to explain or give reasons for something. Start your answer with the word **'because'**, like this:

Why didn't Oscar like fishing?

because it was hard work and he was lazy

Take time to think

You need to think carefully to answer a why question.

You still have to find the right part of the story. But the answer is not there right in front of you. You cannot just copy the answer. Instead you must use your own words.

You need to think about what you read. Then you can work out the reason from what the story tells you.

Test yourself!

Answer the questions on this page about the story 'Fair shares'.

Remember

To answer a **why** question, start with the word **'because'**. Make sure your reason comes from something in the story.

What do you think?

Sometimes you need to think about the whole story. For example, you might think about the main idea of the story or how well the story worked. You may be asked questions that ask for your ideas. Here are some examples:

What do you think the story tells us?

What do you think will happen now?

What do you like or not like about the story?

All these questions ask what **you** think. But you must still use things from the story in your answers.

A question about the story 'Fair shares'

This question is about the story on page 9.

Do you think Oscar will be pleased with his brother? Why or why not?

Look back to page 9 and decide how you would answer. Think about each character and about all the events in the story to help you answer. Remember that the question asks you why, so you must give a **reason**:

No, I do not think Oscar will be pleased. Not when he realises that he has done all the work, but got no fish!

Test yourself!

Think again about the story on page 9. Answer these questions.

1. Do you think 'Clever Oscar' would be another good title for the story? Give a reason for your answer.
2. Do you think what Bruno did to his brother was fair? Give a reason to explain your answer.
3. Did you enjoy the story? Give a reason.

Remember

Say what you think, but use **something in the story** to explain your ideas.

Thinking about characters

Stories are about characters and the things that happen to them. A story tells you a lot about the main characters. It tells you who the characters are, what they look like and what sort of people they are.

How to find out about the people in a story

Find words that tell you or show you things

When you read a story, look for words that **tell you** about a character. For example:

Otto the fruit seller was poor but happy.

Other words will **show you** how characters feel or what they are thinking. For example:

Otto frowned as he stood beneath the tree looking up into the branches. Now he had hurt his back, he could no longer climb up to get the best fruit.

Find out what the characters do and say

The characters' actions and words can show what sort of people they are. For example:

"Let me help you with that," said Otto, taking up the old man's heavy load.

Try reading the characters' minds!

Imagine a thought bubble coming from each character's mind. Think about what he or she is thinking.

Test yourself!

Read again about Otto, and answer these questions.

1. What was Otto's job?
2. What sort of person was Otto? How can you tell?
3. Why is Otto worried when he has a bad back?

Remember

Look for details that **tell you about** the characters. Think about what they **say** and **do**.

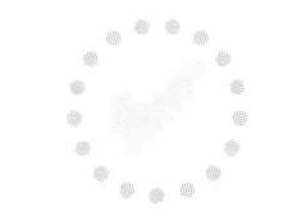

Reading a non-fiction text

A fiction text tells us a made-up story. A non-fiction text gives us information or facts about something.

There are lots of different types of non-fiction texts. Here are some examples.

an information book

a newspaper

a recipe

a dictionary

a football match programme

a letter

Different ways of reading non-fiction texts

- You might read a non-fiction text from start to finish. You start at the beginning and read until you get to the end.

But sometimes you just choose bits to read.

- You might skim through. Skimming means looking quickly through the text to find out what it is about.
- You might be looking for something and scan the text to find key words.

Test yourself!

Answer these questions about the non-fiction texts at the top of the page.

1 Which **two** should you read from the beginning to the end?

2 Which **one** would you **never** read from the beginning to the end?

Remember

We can read non-fiction texts in different ways. Sometimes we read right through. Sometimes we **skim** or **scan** to find bits to read.

Features of non-fiction texts

Non-fiction texts are set out so that it is easy to find the information you want.

Finding information in a book

Non-fiction books often have a **contents** page at the front and an **index** at the back. These help you find the pages you need.

Contents

Dogs	2
Cats	4
Rabbits	6
Mice	8
Fish	10
Snakes	11
Birds	12

The contents page tells you what is on each page of the book.

Index

birds 12, 13	hutch 7
cage 12	lead 3
cats 4, 5	mice 8, 9
dogs 2, 3	rabbits 6, 7
exercise 3	snakes 11
fish 10	tank 10

The index gives a list of subjects and their page numbers. The index is in **alphabetical order** to help you find a word quickly.

Finding information on a page

Each page in a non-fiction book is set out to help you find information quickly. Look for:

- a **heading** or **sub-heading**, which tells you what a page or section is about
- a list of **bullet points** to make each point stand out
- a **text box** that makes one bit of information stand out from the rest of the text.

Remember

Non-fiction texts are set out in special ways to help you to find information.

Test yourself!

1. Why are ingredients in a recipe set out as a list?
2. Why are words in a dictionary set out in alphabetical order?
3. Why does this book have a heading at the top of each page?

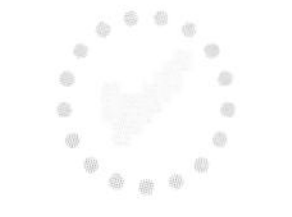

Finding answers

Scanning

You might read a non-fiction text to find the answer to a question. If you scan through the text, this can help you to find the answer quickly.

Imagine that you wanted to answer this question.

What do caterpillars eat?

Here is some information about caterpillars to help you answer the question:

Caterpillars are the young of butterflies. They hatch out of eggs. Caterpillars feed on leaves and other parts of plants. They eat a lot so that they grow bigger. When they are fully grown they spin a cocoon.

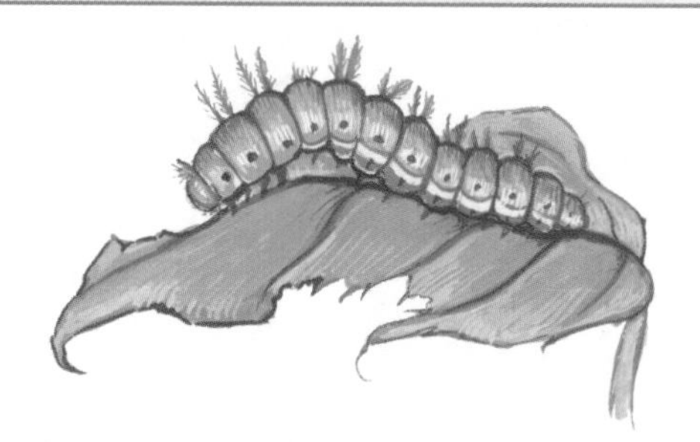

How to scan the text – and find the answer quickly!

1. **Read the question** and underline the key words.

   What do caterpillars eat?

2. **Scan the text** to find the key words or words that mean the same.

   Caterpillars feed on leaves and other parts of plants.

   You might not find exactly the same words. Notice that 'feed on' means the same as 'eat'.

3. Read the whole sentence to **find the answer**.

   Caterpillars feed on leaves and other parts of plants.

If you do not find the answer first time, scan for the key words again. Or read the sentences before and after.

Test yourself!

Use the information about caterpillars to answer these questions.

1. What are caterpillars?
2. Why do caterpillars eat a lot?
3. When do caterpillars spin a cocoon?

Remember

Scan for **key words** to help you find answers quickly.

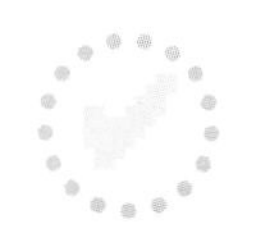

Information in pictures

It is not only words that give information. Pictures give information too!
A non-fiction book might have photographs, drawings, diagrams or charts.

Photographs and drawings

Photographs and drawings can show you what something looks like.

Always read the caption that goes with a picture. The caption tells you what the picture shows. It can also give you extra information.

Butterflies feed on nectar from flowers.

Diagrams

A diagram shows something in detail. Always read the labels on a diagram. The labels point out important parts or features.

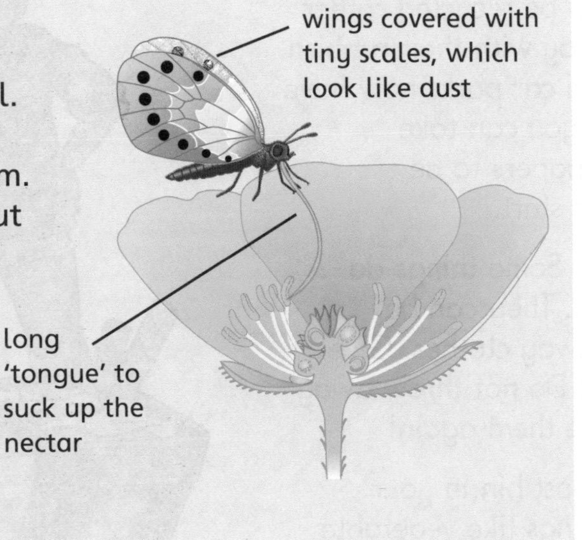

Charts

Some information may be set out in a **chart** or **table**. This makes it easier for the reader to pick out key **facts** quickly.

	Butterfly	Wasp	Ladybird
Length in centimetres (cm)	4 to 5 cm	2 cm	Half a cm

Test yourself!

1 What are a butterfly's wings covered with?
2 How does a butterfly suck up nectar?
3 What do butterflies feed on?
4 What does the chart tell us about butterflies?

Remember

Always read **captions** and **labels** on diagrams or pictures.

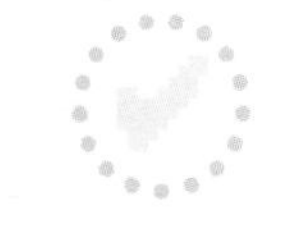

Information text

Read this information carefully. Think about it as you read.

The great recycle

Every week we fill our bins with rubbish. We put our bins out and the rubbish is taken away.

Some of the rubbish is dumped in huge holes in the ground. It rots and gives off smelly gases. Some of the rubbish is burned. It makes smoke that fills the air. This is all bad for the **environment**.

Even worse we throw away useful materials like metal and glass that can be **recycled**. Think about all the paper you throw away every day. Paper can be recycled and made into new paper. This means we do not have to cut down more trees to make more paper.

Recycle and reuse!

Many people now have a recycling box where they put things that can be recycled rather than throwing them away with their rubbish. Many supermarkets and car parks now have recycling points where you can take bottles, cans and newspapers to be recycled. This is a good start.

But you could do more! Some things do not need to be recycled. They can be **reused**. Do not throw away clothes. Give them to a charity shop! Do not throw away plastic carrier bags. Use them again!

You might have a compost bin in your garden. You can put things like vegetable peelings in the compost bin rather than in your rubbish bin. Your waste helps to feed the plants.

Join the great recycle! Recycle, reuse and make a difference!

Glossary

environment: the land, sea and air around us

recycled: made into something else, like new

reused: used again

Thinking about the facts

Sometimes you need to do more reading to find the information you want. Sometimes you need to stop and think about what you have read.

Read more

You might need more than one piece of information. It might be in different places on the page.

Read these questions about the **text** on page 18:

1 a) What **three** materials are easy to recycle?
b) What can you do to make sure there is less rubbish in your bin? Write down **three** things.

You need several pieces of information for your answers. The information you need is not all in one place. You must look, read, and then read more.

Stop and think

Reading **non-fiction** is not just about finding information. You also need to think about it.

Read these questions. They will help you to think about the text on page 18.

2 a) Why do you think it is important to recycle?
b) How can you tell that more people are now recycling?
c) Choose one thing your family could recycle.
d) Why did you choose this thing?

You need to think about the information in 'The great recycle' to answer these questions. Don't forget to give reasons for your answers.

Test yourself!

Read 'The great recycle'. Then answer questions 1 and 2 in the boxes on this page.

Remember

You need to read an information text carefully. You need to **think about** the ideas in the text.

Reading a poem

Poems are special. They have a special shape and a special sound. They look different and sound different to other sorts of writing.

Listen to the sound of a poem

Find a poem. Read it aloud. Listen for the special sound patterns made by the words.
For example:

- Listen for words that **rhyme**. They have the same sound at the end.

  Summer <u>sun</u>
  Let's have <u>fun</u>

- Listen for words that begin with the same letter sound.

  <u>S</u>izzling <u>s</u>ummer <u>s</u>un

- Listen for the **rhythm** or beat in the poem. The rhythm will make your toes tap!

  Sun, sun, sun –
  Let's have fun!

Look at the shape of the poem

Look at how the **poet** has set out the poem on the page. Here are some ideas to help you.

- Look at the shape of the poem.
- See if it is split into verses.
- Are any words or lines used more than once?
- Is there any one word on a line by itself?

Test yourself!

Slow, slow,
Said the snail.
Slowly laying
His slippery trail.

Busy, busy,
Said the bee.
Buzzing by
Buzzzzzzzzzzily.

Look at the poem above:

1. Write down two words that rhyme with each other in the first verse.
2. Write down three words that begin with the same letter sound in the second verse.
3. How does the last word of the poem stand out?

Remember

Use your **ears** to hear the **sound patterns** of a poem. Use your **eyes** to look at the **shape** of a poem.

Thinking about a poem

Do not read a poem just once. Read it a few times! Each time you read the poem, think about what it says. Think about the main idea and what it tells you. Think about each word and what you learn from it.

Read a poem again and again

Each time you read the poem you will notice more details. You will understand the poem better. The poem might make you think or feel in a special way.

Look carefully at every word

A poet chooses words very carefully. Each word is important to the meaning of the poem. So when you read a poem, think about the words and what they say to you.

For example, if one line in a poem reads:

Raindrops explode on the window pane

... then you might ask yourself, "Why does the poet use the word 'explode'?"

What is this poem about?

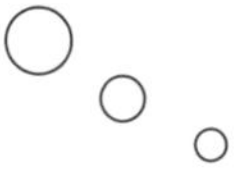

Rain

The rain is falling all around
It falls on field and tree,
It rains on the umbrellas here
And on the ships at sea.

By **Robert Louis Stevenson**

What pictures does the poem make in my mind?

What does it make me think about?

Test yourself!

Questions can help you think about a poem. Some questions help you to notice small details. Other questions check that you understand the ideas.

Read the poem 'Rain'. Then answer these questions about it.

1 The poem says that the rain falls on four things. What are these four things?

2 What is the main idea in this poem?

Remember

Read a poem a few times and think about the main idea.

Writing in sentences

When we write we usually put each of our ideas into a sentence. Every sentence tells the reader one of our ideas. All sentences must:

- ✔ make sense
- ✔ give one complete idea
- ✔ have a capital letter at the start and a full stop at the end.

You can write more sentences to add more ideas. For example:

Apples are crispy. They are good for you. Try eating an apple a day.

How to write a sentence

1. **Say the whole sentence** in your head before you write it down.
2. Put a **capital letter** at the start of the first word.
3. As you write, **say the sentence word by word** in your head.
4. **Add a full stop at the end**, when you have written the last word.
5. Read the sentence to **check it makes sense**.

Test yourself!

Write three sentences about your favourite game or sport. Use a different colour pen or pencil for each sentence.

Remember

When you write, **think in sentences**. Say each sentence in your head before you write it down.

Linking ideas together

You can put two ideas or two pieces of information into one sentence. You just need to use one of these special linking words:

and *but* *so*

These words let you carry on a sentence. After the linking word you can add another idea or another piece of information.

Idea 1	Linking word	Idea 2
The Queen stood up	*and*	*everyone cheered.*
We set off early	*but*	*the bus was late.*
It began to rain	*so*	*we went back inside.*

How to use linking words in a sentence

1. Say the **whole sentence** in your head before you write it down.
2. **Write the first idea** but **do not put a full stop** at the end. Instead, **write the linking word.**
3. Then write the second idea.
4. **Add a full stop** at the end.

If you have a lot of ideas, it is good to use some linking words. For example:

> Apples are crispy and have smooth skins. They are good for you, so try eating an apple a day.

Test yourself!

A linking word has been added to each of the sentences below. Add another idea to carry on the sentence.

1. It was hot **so**
2. Jack ran away **but**
3. The phone rang **and**

Remember

Use the words **'and'**, **'but'** and **'so'** to link two ideas in one sentence.

More linking words

Here are two more special linking words:

because when

These words can help you to write a longer sentence. They let you write a main idea and then say more about it.

Using the word 'because'

You can use the word because to give a reason or explain an idea.

You might write down a main idea, like this:

It is important to do some exercise every day

Then you should give a reason to explain your idea. Write the word because and you can carry on the sentence, like this:

It is important to do some exercise every day because it keeps you fit and healthy.

Using the word 'when'

You can use the word when to say more about **when** something happened.

Look at how this sentence carries on after the word when:

We went out to play when it stopped raining.

Test yourself!

Carry on each of these sentences:

1. A dictionary is very useful **because**
2. Joe was in a hurry **because**
3. The ice started to melt **because**
4. Ben was happy **when**
5. We went to bed **when**

Remember

Use **'because'** to give a reason. Use **'when'** to say when something happened.

Interesting sentences

Make some of your sentences more interesting by adding extra information. Try this when you think of a sentence in your head.

Start with a simple sentence like this:

Joe went for a walk.

This simple sentence is fine. But you could tell the reader where Joe went. You can add this detail to the **end** of the sentence:

Joe went for a walk in the park.

... or you could tell the reader when he went. Add this to the **start** of the sentence:

After breakfast, Joe went for a walk.

... or you could tell the reader how he went. Add this to **the middle** of the sentence:

Joe quickly went for a walk.

... or you could use the word because and tell the reader **why** he went:

Joe went for a walk because he wanted to think.

You could even give the reader all this detail in one sentence!

After breakfast, Joe quickly went for a walk in the park because he wanted to think.

Test yourself!

Add more information to these sentences:

1 Dan rode his bike. (When? Where?)

2 Carrie slipped out of the door. (When? How?)

3 The dog ran. (Where? How?)

Remember

You can put several pieces of information in one sentence. Write sentences that say **where, when** or **how** things happened.

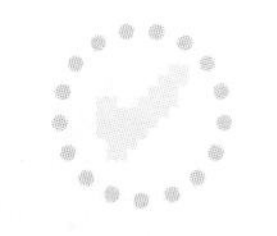

Colourful sentences

A sentence can sound dull and boring. You can make dull sentences more colourful and more interesting by adding describing words.

Describing things

Describing words tell you more about people and things. They give detail and make a better picture. Take a dull sentence like:

A man lived in a cottage.

You can add describing words to say more about the man and the cottage:

A lonely old man lived in a tiny, run-down cottage.

The describing words help to bring the sentence to life.

Describing actions

Some describing words describe actions or say how events happen. Picture this colourful scene:

The goggle-eyed alien ran after the big, shaggy dog.

Now you can make it even more colourful, like this:

The goggle-eyed alien ran clumsily after the big, shaggy dog.

The word clumsily adds to the picture. It tells us how the alien ran.

Test yourself!

Add some describing words to make these sentences more colourful:

1. The lady was wearing a hat.
2. The wolf climbed the tree.
3. Waves crashed onto the rocks.

Remember

Use **describing words** to give a clearer picture of **things, people** and **events**.

Types of non-fiction writing

Sometimes when we write, we are telling people about something or giving information. This is called non-fiction writing. There are lots of different types of non-fiction writing.

Here are some non-fiction writing tasks:

Write instructions to tell others how to play your favourite game.

Imagine you are on holiday. Write a postcard to your best friend.

Write a letter to a new pen-friend.

Write about a school trip for your school magazine or web page.

Write a report or information booklet about your favourite hobby.

Making a start

Always start by thinking about texts you have read. If you want to write a letter, think about letters you have read. If you want to write instructions, think about instructions you have used.

- Picture how the text was **set out** on the page.
- Think about what it **told** you.
- Remember how it **sounded**.

Then make your own writing look and sound similar!

Test yourself!

Look at the writing tasks on this page. For each task, think of something you have read that would help you to do that piece of writing.

Remember

Think about a text you have read, how it was **set out**, what it **said** and how it **sounded**. Use it to help you with your writing.

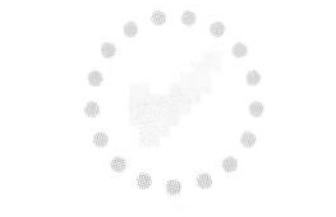

Stop, think and organise!

Do not just start writing. Your ideas will be all mixed up. Your writing will not make sense. Always stop, think and organise.

Stop and think

Think about what you are going to write.
The three 'big' things to think about are:

- how to start
- what to write in the middle
- how to end.

Organise events

If you are writing about events that happen in an order, think through this order carefully. For example, you might write the ideas as a flowchart:

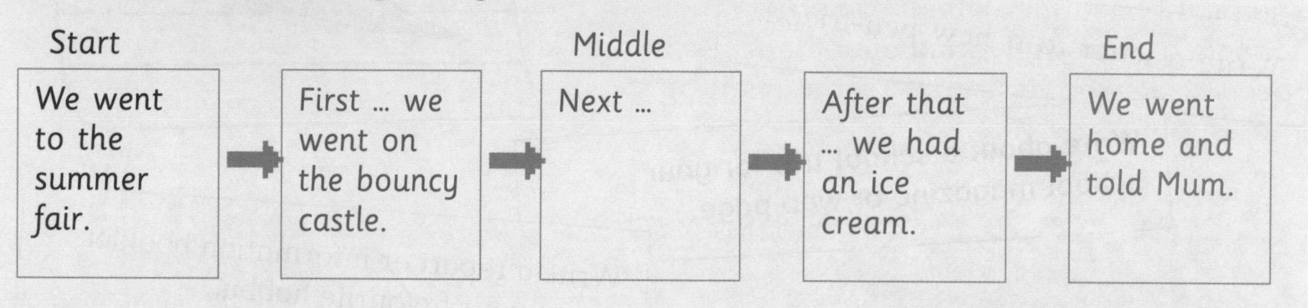

Organise information

If you want to give information about a topic, think about all the different bits that you want to put in.

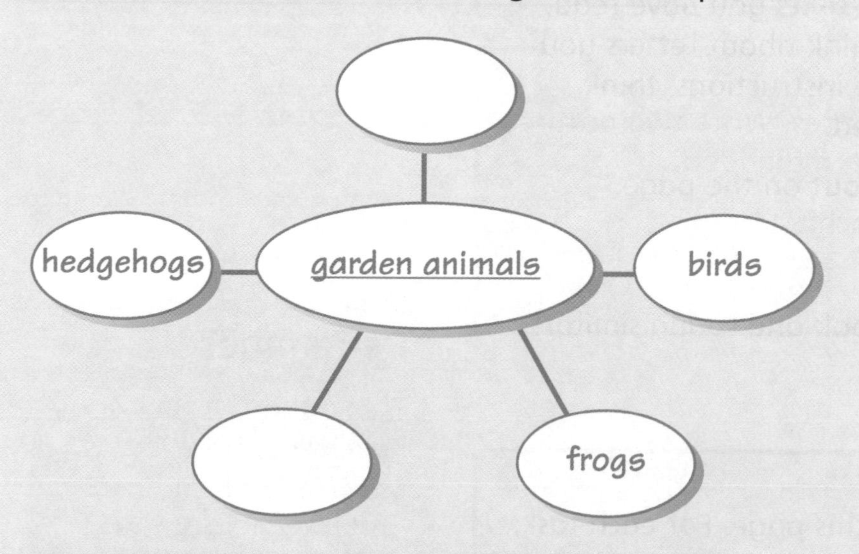

This is a planning star. The main topic goes in the middle.
The things you want to write about go round the outside.

Test yourself!

1 Add another event to the middle box in the flowchart.
2 Add two more ideas to the 'garden animals' planning star.

Remember

Stop, think and **organise** before you start writing.

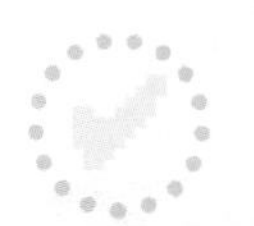

Adding detail

When you start writing, add interesting details to your main ideas.

Imagine that you are writing about the topic **'Hedgehogs'**. You start by writing a **main idea** sentence like this:

Hedgehogs are small animals with spikes.

Then you think of some interesting details about hedgehogs and write two or three more sentences.

Hedgehogs are small animals with spikes. They eat slugs and other insects. They roll up into a ball when they are scared or in danger.

Describe something that happened

You might be writing about something that happened. Start by writing a main idea sentence. Then decide what else your reader might find interesting:

First we went on the bouncy castle.
It was great fun bouncing all over the place.
Dad said we looked like mad kangaroos!

Add details about the events.
Use **description** to bring it alive.
Say how you or others reacted to the events.

Test yourself!

Here are two **main idea** sentences. Write two or three more sentences to follow each main idea.

1 We had a picnic on the beach.

2 An ant is an insect.

Remember

Write a **main idea** and then write some more sentences that give interesting **details** about it.

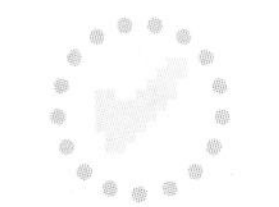

How does it sound?

When you read a non-fiction text, you can hear the sound of the **writer's voice**.

Sometimes the writer's voice sounds chatty, as in a postcard or a friendly letter:

Do you remember when Dad fell in the pool? Wasn't it funny!

Sometimes the writer's voice sounds bossy, as when giving instructions:

Now close the lid carefully.

Sometimes the writer's voice sounds formal and polite, as in an invitation to a grand event:

The Queen of Hearts requests the pleasure of your company.

Using the right voice

When you write non-fiction, you need to use the right sort of voice. It helps to think of something you have read. Think about how it sounded. Make your writing sound similar.

- Try saying things in your head before you write them.
- Imagine yourself saying things in the 'writer's voice'.
- When you have finished, read your writing through. Check that it sounds right.

Test yourself!

What voice would you use for writing:

1 a postcard to your best friend?

2 a letter to someone very important?

3 instructions for how to keep the classroom tidy?

Remember

Think about how your writing **sounds** as well as what you write.

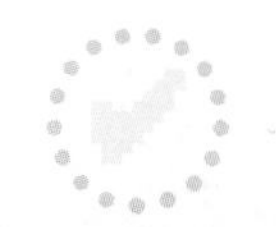

The right word

When you are writing information, it is important to use the right words. You need to think about the words you use. Choose the best, most exact words for the topic. Here are some examples.

If you are writing about the topic **'Growing plants'**, use topic words such as:

shoot	root	seedling	compost

If you are writing a recipe, use the kinds of words found in recipes, such as:

slice	mix	chop	stir

Choosing the right word

The first word that comes into your head might not be quite the right word for that sentence. Stop and think of the exact word before you write it down.

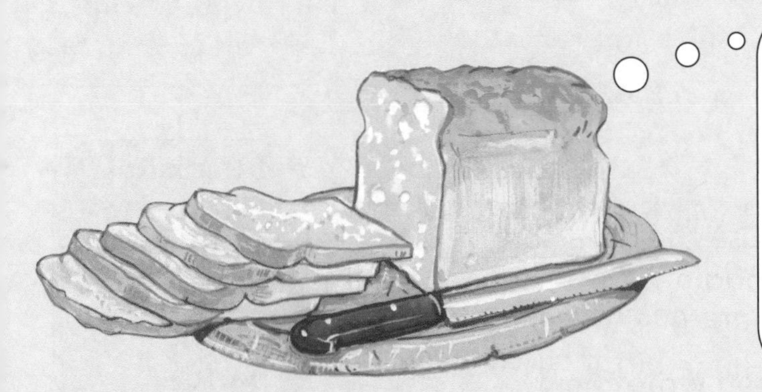

Slice the bread into thin bits.

'bits' is not the right word! I need an exact word. I know:

Slice the bread into thin strips.

'strips' is a better word because it says exactly how to slice the bread.

Test yourself!

One word in each sentence is underlined. It is not the right word to use. Think of a better word to go in the sentence.

1 <u>Bits</u> of snow began to fall.

2 Fill the flowerpot with <u>dirt</u>.

3 The lolly stick <u>stayed</u> on the water.

Remember

Non-fiction writing needs **exact words**. Think carefully about the words you use.

Writing a letter

There are lots of reasons for writing **letters**. You can write **chatty letters** to friends to tell them your news. You can write **formal letters** to people you do not know to ask them things.

Here is a chatty letter from Beth. She is inviting her friend Ross to a party. The yellow stickers show you what Beth was thinking when she wrote each part of the letter.

Letters are set out with the address and date at the top.

15 Green Lane
Belton
BE1 9GT

1st June

Letters start with the word 'Dear'

Dear Ross

This sounds a friendly way to start.

Sorry to hear about your cold. I hope you are feeling better.

Now I must tell Ross why I am writing.

I have really exciting news. I am having a party on Friday 16th June. Mum says you can come as long as it is OK with your stepdad. I do hope you can come.

I think Ross will like to hear about my plans for the party.

All my friends from school will be here. We will all have balloons. We are going to have the paddling pool if it is sunny. There are going to be lots of fun games and I will have a huge birthday cake.

Please say you can come. It starts at 5 o'clock and it is at my house.

Friendly letters often end like this.

Hope to see you then!

Best wishes, from

Beth

Write a letter from Goldilocks inviting Baby Bear to her party.

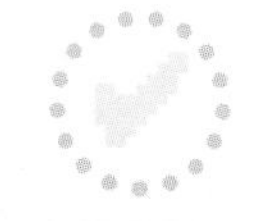

Writing a recount

In a **recount**, you write about events or **something that happened**.

Here is Umar's recount of his day out at a summer fair. The yellow stickers show you what Umar was thinking when he wrote the recount.

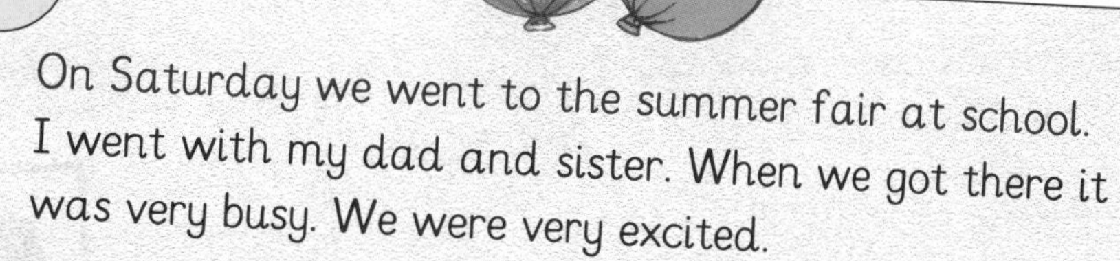

My first sentence says what I am writing about.

On Saturday we went to the summer fair at school. I went with my dad and sister. When we got there it was very busy. We were very excited.

Now, I must write about the events in order.

First, we went on the bouncy castle. It was great fun bouncing all over the place. Dad said we looked like mad kangaroos!

I will put this in because it is funny.

Next we went round all the stalls and had a go at all the games. I won a football in the penalty shoot-out game.

'Next' is a good linking word.

After that we were very hot so we had an ice cream. The ice cream was melting fast. Mine went all down my arm. My sister got ice cream on her T-shirt. We did look a mess!

This is quite funny too. I think the reader will like it.

When we got home we gave Mum a balloon and told her all about our great day out.

This sounds like the end.

Test yourself!

Write a recount of a special day that you can remember well.

Writing a postcard and writing a diary

Postcards and diaries are like recounts. You write about things that have happened or things you have done. But postcards and diaries are both set out in special ways.

A postcard

We send **postcards** to tell our friends about **what we have been doing** on **holiday**. A postcard is set out like this:

Postcards start with a **friendly informal greeting**.

There is only room for **a few interesting details**.

The **end** of a postcard sounds a bit like a **letter**.

2nd August

Hi there!

We are having a great time in Sea Town. We are staying right by the beach and I've been in the sea every day. Mum says I will turn into a mermaid!

See you when I get back.

Love,

Jen

Miss Katie Fellows
15 Green Street
Singham
BE20 9BS

A diary

We write a **diary** to keep a **record** of **interesting things we do.** A diary is set out like this:

I have written about something interesting that happened on each day.

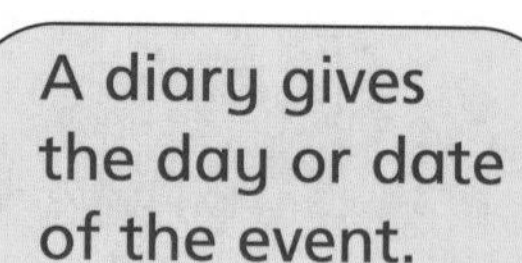

My holiday diary

Saturday 29 July

Terrible journey! We were stuck in a traffic jam for over an hour! But we are here now and the caravan site is great. The beach is so close you can hear the sea.

Sunday 30 July

Jack and I spent the whole day playing on the beach.

Test yourself!

Write another two sentences in Jen's holiday diary for Sunday.

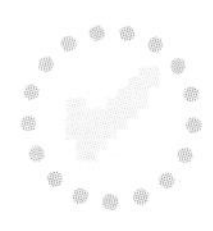

Writing a report

You write a **report** to **tell people about something**. The information has to be **organised** to go in the report. You can organise the information using headings. Sometimes you break up the text with a sub-heading.

Here is a report that Tarun wrote about animals found in the garden. The yellow stickers show you what Tarun was thinking when he wrote the report.

My heading says what the report is about.

Animals in the garden

You will find lots of animals living in your garden if you look closely.

This sounds like a good first sentence.

<u>Hedgehogs</u>
Hedgehogs are small animals with spikes. They eat slugs and other insects. A hedgehog rolls up into a ball when it is scared or in danger.

The sub-headings tell the reader what each bit is about.

I will put in some interesting things about hedgehogs.

<u>Frogs</u>
Frogs are usually green or brown. They like to live near water and they eat flies and slugs. Frogs start off as tadpoles living in the water and then change into frogs.

Now I need to write a few sentences about frogs.

<u>Birds</u>

Test yourself!

Write three or four sentences under the heading **'Birds'** for the report on **'Animals in the garden'**.

Writing instructions

You write **instructions** to tell someone **how to do something**. For example, you might tell someone how to **make something**, how to **get somewhere** or how to **play a game**.

Here are the instructions for making a jam sandwich. The thought bubbles show you what Ellie was thinking when she wrote them.

I will start the heading 'How to ...'
That sounds like a heading for instructions.

You will need

- 2 slices of bread
- margarine
- jam.

A recipe starts with a list like this.

This is what you do.

1 Spread the margarine thinly over the two slices of bread.

2 Put a spoonful of jam on one slice of bread and spread it out.

3 Place the other slice on top.

4 Carefully cut the sandwich into quarters.

I must tell the reader what to do, so I will start 'Spread ...'

I will put each step on a new line so it is easy to follow.

Instructions often have numbers to show the order.

This diagram will show the reader how to cut the sandwich.

Now you can enjoy your jam sandwich.

Test yourself!

Imagine you have some sunflower seeds. Write instructions for how to grow a giant sunflower.

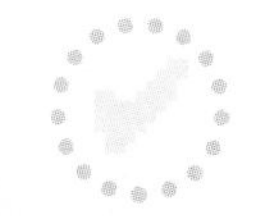

Thinking of ideas

When you write a **story**, start by thinking about stories you have read. Think about what the stories are about and how they sound. This will help you write a story of your own.

Ideas and an opening

A story you have read might give you an idea for something to write about. Or it might help you think of a way to begin your story.

Special story ingredients

Think about the three special ingredients in a story:

- each **character** (who is in the story)
- the **setting** (where and when the story takes place)
- the **events** (what happens and why).

Test yourself!

Think of ideas for a story called 'The three wishes'. Start by thinking about fairy tales and traditional stories you know. Write down ideas for two characters, a setting and some events.

Make it sound like a story!

What kind of **language** should you use? Think how other stories sound. Keep the sound in your head and make your story sound similar.

Remember

You can get ideas for characters, settings, events and story language by thinking about stories you have read.

Planning the story

It is a good idea to think through your whole **story** before you start writing. Think about how your story will begin ... what will happen in the middle ... and how it will end.

Think of your story as a **storyboard** like this:

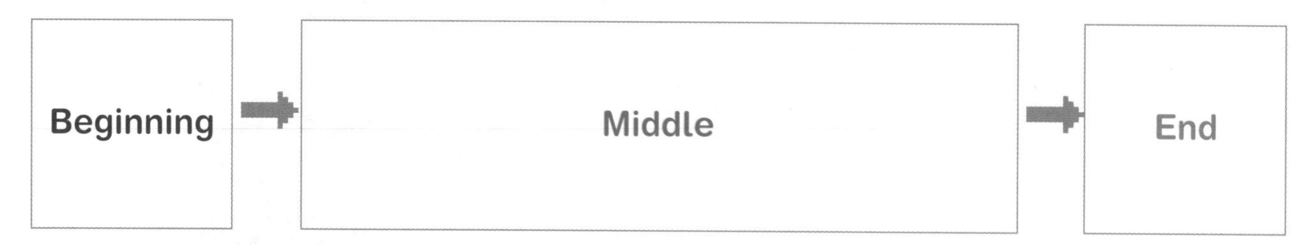

You might have lots of things happening in the middle of your story. So add more boxes in the middle of your storyboard.

Deciding what happens

Think through the story **events** in order.
You can do this in your head. Or you can make **notes** or a plan, like this.

Beginning: *Josh found torch in shed.*

↓

Middle: *Torch light shone on wooden box.*

↓

Box was full of treasure!

↓

Josh gave the treasure to his friends.

↓

End: *Everyone happy. Josh kept the torch.*

↓

Test yourself!

Make a plan or storyboard for one of these story titles:

'The giant pizza'

'Helpful Harry'

'Don't get lost!'

Remember

Think through the **beginning, middle** and **end** of your story before you start writing.

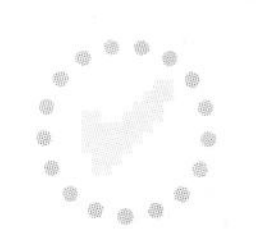

Using time links

In a story, everything must happen in the right order. One thing happens. **Then** something else happens! **Then** something else again, and so on ...

But it sounds boring if you keep writing

and then ... and then ... and then

Instead you can put a full stop and start a new sentence with a special linking word or phrase. These special linking words join events together.

How to use linking words

Here are some examples of linking words:

Once ... In an instant ... Later ... Meanwhile ...

Some linking words say when events happened:

Early one morning ... The next day ...
Later that night ...

Some linking words show that something happened a long time later:

Eventually ... After a long time ... Finally ...

Some linking words show that something happened quickly:

All of a sudden ... Just then ... At that moment ...

Each time you write about a new event in your story, remember to start with a linking word.

Test yourself!

Write what happened next, after the linking words.

1. Cinderella sat down and began to cry. **All of a sudden ...**
2. Jack climbed, and climbed, and climbed. **Eventually ...**
3. Hansel and Gretel fell fast asleep in the forest. **The next morning ...**

Remember

Do not write **'and then'**. Instead put a full stop and start a new sentence with a linking word or phrase.

The details of the story

When you write a story, try to make it as interesting as the stories you read in books. Story writers add details and description to keep readers interested. You can do this too. Add details about the events to bring your story to life. Think like a real story writer. Your stories will be gripping!

How to write good stories

Here are some ideas to help you write better stories.

- Describe the setting so readers can picture the place. For example:

  The woods were dark and overgrown.

- Add details about each character. Show who the characters are, what they look like and how they feel. For example:

  Everyone knew old Mr Cooper and his amazing hats! or
  The princess sighed and a tear ran down her face.

- Add something funny or exciting to make your reader want to keep reading. For example:

  Splash! Something landed in the water next to her.

- Use some special story language. For example:

  It was a great big golden pizza!

- Keep the storyteller's voice in your head as you write. Try out ideas to see how they sound before you write them down.

Test yourself!

Make this event more interesting by adding details, description or story language:

Then Harry saw something in the sea.

Remember

Think like a storyteller. Use **details** and **description** to make your story sound like a story in a book.

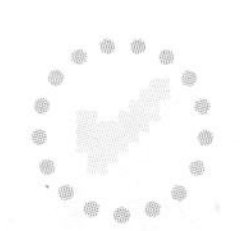

Finding the best word

Choose the best words to describe things in your story. Interesting words make your writing better.

How to find words that make an impact

Do not use the first word that comes into your head.

Stop and think! Ask yourself:
Is there a more interesting or better word?

There are lots of exciting words that mean the same as 'shone'. For example:

Try a few words in your head before you choose one. Think of an interesting word rather than a boring one. Try to think of the **best** word rather than an everyday word. For example, do not use the everyday word **'looked'** when you could use:

stared gazed peeped glared glimpsed

Decide which one is the best word for your story.

Test yourself!

Think of a better word to use in place of the underlined word:

1 The little mouse looked round the corner.

2 The cake was nice.

3 "Please let me go!" said the tiny alien.

Remember

Do not use the first word that comes into your head. Choose the best, most interesting word.

Checking your writing

When you are writing, stop every now and then. Go back to the start and read your story right through. Check that it makes sense and sounds right. If something sounds odd, change it.

When did the events happen?

In a story we usually write as if events have already happened, in the past. We write in the past tense. For example:

Josh went and looked in the garden shed.

But sometimes you might forget. You might suddenly start writing as if things are happening now, as you watch! For example:

Josh turns the key and carefully opens the lid.

When you re-read your story, listen for sudden changes from the past to the present. Change the words so that you keep to the same time. For example:

Josh turned the key and carefully opened the lid.

Who is the story about?

When you start writing you choose a main character. Here the main character is Josh.

Josh peeked inside. He gasped.

But you might forget about Josh half way through and use the word 'I' by mistake.

Josh peeked inside. He gasped. I was amazed.

When you re-read your story, check this out. Change the word 'I' if necessary. Here we could change 'I' to 'Josh' or 'He'.

Test yourself!

Change the words so it sounds as though these events have already happened.

1 It is 12 o'clock. Cinderella runs out of the palace.

2 The monster is close by. Alex listens for his footsteps.

Remember

Re-read your story in your head to check that everything sounds right.

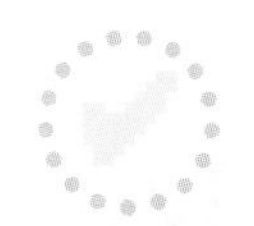

Writing a poem

Why not try writing a simple poem of your own? Just follow the steps below.

Think about your subject

Before you start writing, think about the subject. Write down words and ideas that come into your head.

For example, to write a poem about ice cream, write down words such as:

cornet
strawberry scoop
chocolate chip
smooth
creamy
vanilla
juice
raspberry ripple
melting
biscuit
rocky road
chilled
wafer
ice-cold

Write some lines

Look at the words and start to make up lines for your poem. You do not need to write every line as a **sentence**. You can make a line from just a few words that go well together. But do not forget to give the first word of each line a **capital** letter.

Always choose the most interesting words or words that sound good together.

Shape and finish your poem

Move your ideas around so that your poem starts to take shape. You might:

- put ideas into verses
- make your poem **rhyme**
- use the same line more than once.

Before you finish, read your poem aloud to make sure it sounds good!

Ice cream

Raspberry ripple
Chocolate chip
Rocky road
Strawberry dip.

Squirt of juice
Toffee swirl
Have a wafer or
A biscuit curl.

Scoop it out
One two three
Cornet for you
Tub for me.

Test yourself!

Read the poem 'Ice cream'. Then write a poem of your own about pizza, sweets or another sort of food.

Remember

Poems need **sound patterns**. Choose words that sound good together.

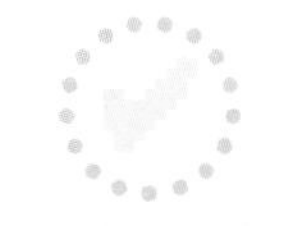

Full stops and capital letters

Every sentence you write needs a capital letter at the start and a full stop at the end.

Why do we need capital letters and full stops?

These important punctuation marks are like signals to the reader.

- A capital letter at the start of a sentence says, "Go!"

We went into the playground.

- A full stop at the end of a sentence says, "Stop!"

We went into the playground.

If there are no full stops and capital letters it is hard to know where to stop and start.

> We went into the playground on the grass there was a climbing frame with a rope ladder next to it was a sand pit

Using full stops and capital letters

Think of a sentence in your head before you write. Then start writing. Put the capital letter, write the sentence and add the full stop.

Check your writing when you have finished. Read your writing aloud in your head. Listen out for where each sentence starts and ends. Check that the full stops and capital letters are in the right places.

Test yourself!

Copy out the passage about the playground, using three capital letters and three full stops. One of the capital letters is there already.

Remember

Every sentence needs a **capital** letter at the start to say **"Go!"** and a **full stop** at the end to say **"Stop!"**

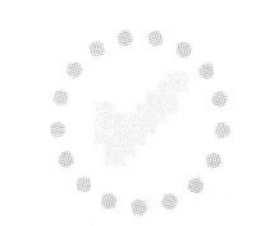

Question marks and exclamation marks

Sometimes a sentence needs a **question mark** or **exclamation mark** rather than a full stop. Question marks and exclamation marks say to the reader: "Look! This is a special sort of sentence."

A question mark says:

This sentence is asking something.

Read this with a question in your voice.

An exclamation mark says:

This sentence is loud or surprising!

Read this with feeling!

Using question marks

If you write a question, you need to put a question mark at the end.

A question **asks** something. Say it aloud or in your head. You will hear that it sounds like a question. For example:

Do you know when to use question marks?

Using exclamation marks

If you write a sentence that shows surprise or that might be said loudly, put an exclamation mark at the end.

What a surprise!

Test yourself!

Put a question mark or an exclamation mark at the end of these sentences:

1 That is amazing

2 What time is it

3 Can I help you

4 Help, save me

Remember

Questions need a question mark. An exclamation mark shows something that is loud or surprising.

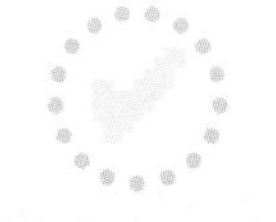

Commas and speech marks

Curly commas

A **comma** looks like a **full stop** with a tail **,**
We use commas to show little breaks in a **sentence**.

You might write a sentence with a list in it. You put a comma after each item in the list to show the breaks.

In the bag there was a bus ticket, a purse, two old photos and a letter.

Speaking with speech marks

We use **speech marks** to show when words are spoken, as when a **character** in a **story** says something.

Think of the character with a speech bubble. What the person says is inside the speech bubble.

Then the speech bubble bursts. Just bits of the bubble are left around the words. These bits are the speech marks:

"How will I ever get home?" cried the girl.

We add the **words at the end** to show who is speaking.

Test yourself!

Put the commas or speech marks into these sentences.

1 Stop! shouted the policeman.

2 I had pizza salad and ice cream for tea.

3 I can help you, said the boy.

4 We play rounders cricket netball and football.

Remember

Speech marks go round words that are spoken. Commas go between items in a list.

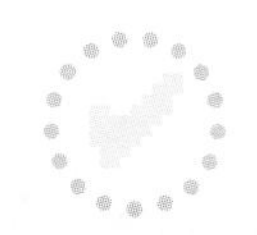

Breaking words down

You can spell lots of short words by breaking them down into sounds or **phonemes**. Breaking down words is sometimes known as **segmenting**. You do it like this.

Say the name of the animal shown in this picture.

Break the word down into sounds or phonemes. Then count the sounds.

There are four phonemes in this word.

Now write the letters that make the sounds. Say each phoneme in turn and write the letter.

___ ___ ___ ___

 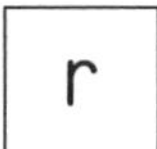  

f r o g

Check by saying the phonemes and building the word: frog!

Two letters make one sound

Sometimes two letters make one sound. Here is an example.

The name of the thing shown in this picture has **four sounds** or phonemes.

But when you write the letters, there are **five letters**.

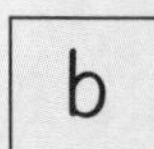 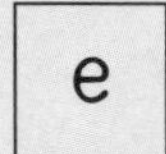 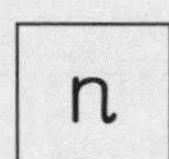 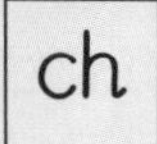

b e n ch

Two letters ('c' and 'h') make one sound ('ch').

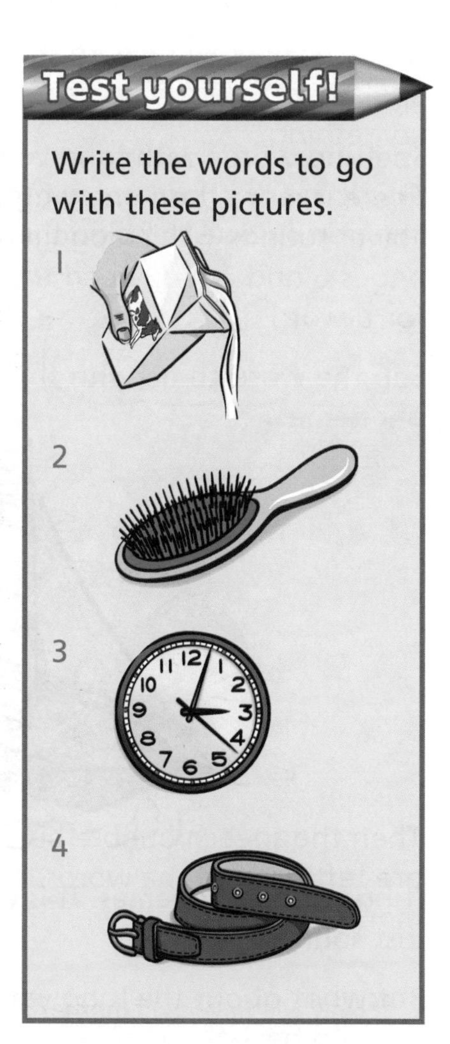

Test yourself!

Write the words to go with these pictures.

1

2

3

4

Remember

You can spell lots of short words by breaking them down into phonemes.

Words with long vowel sounds

Before you read this page, go back to pages 6 and 7. Make sure you know the long **vowel** sounds shown there.

Lots of words have long vowel sounds. Most long vowel sounds need two or more letters to make them. For example:

s p oo n

two letters ('oo') make the long vowel sound in 'spoon'.

Tricky vowel sounds

Spelling words with long vowel sounds can be tricky. There is more than one way to make most long vowel sounds – think again about what you read on pages 6 and 7. You need to know the right spelling for a word.

Say the word to go with this picture. Count the **phonemes**.

It has three phonemes. It is easy to write the first and last sounds: b __ t

But what about the long vowel sound in the middle? It could be:

o-e oa ow oe

You need to know the right spelling for this word.

In the word 'b-oa-t' the long vowel sound is spelt 'oa'.

Test yourself!

Spell the names of the things shown in these pictures. Choose the right spelling of the long vowel sound for each word.

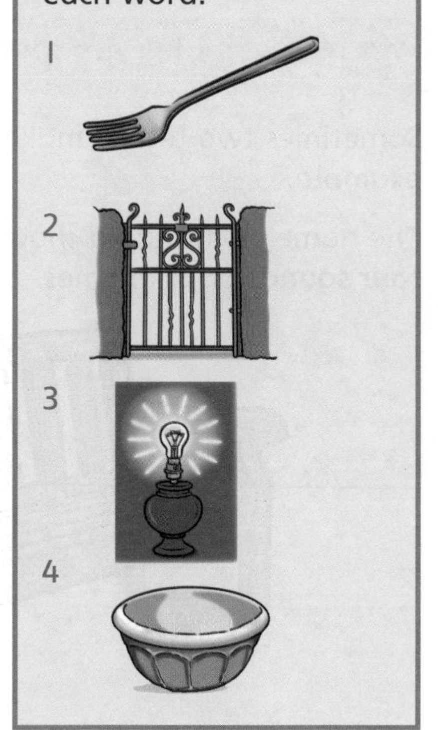

Remember

Long vowel sounds can be tricky. Think about the right spelling for the word you are writing.

Using syllables to help with spelling

Some words are too long to break into phonemes. First you need to break them into syllables.

A **syllable** is a small part of a word. You can hear the syllables when you say the word. They are like the beats in the word.

'afternoon' breaks down into: ➡ 'af-ter-noon' (three syllables)

Counting syllables

You can clap as you say each beat.
Clap and count the syllables in these words:

'important' ➡ 'im-por-tant' (three syllables)

'remembering' ➡ 're-mem-ber-ing' (four syllables)

'hippopotamus' ➡ 'hip-po-pot-a-mus' (five syllables)

Spelling longer words

Say the word as if you are chopping it up into little pieces.

For example:

'holiday' ➡ 'hol-i-day'
'disgusting' ➡ 'dis-gust-ing'
'suddenly' ➡ 'sud-den-ly'

Now it is easier to spell the word because you can write it bit by bit.

Cover the seven long words shown in red on this page. Say the syllables and see if you can write the word without looking at it again.

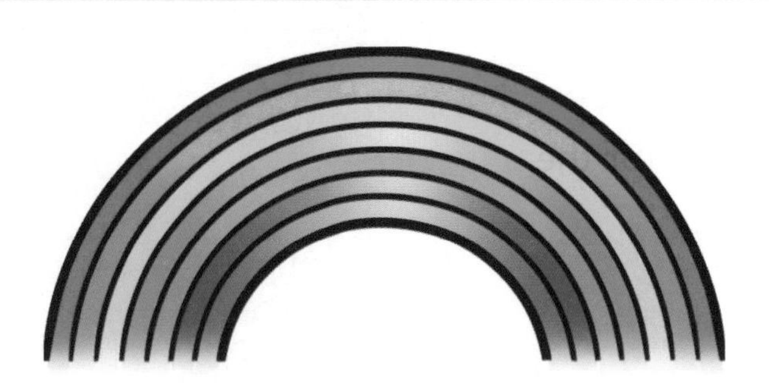

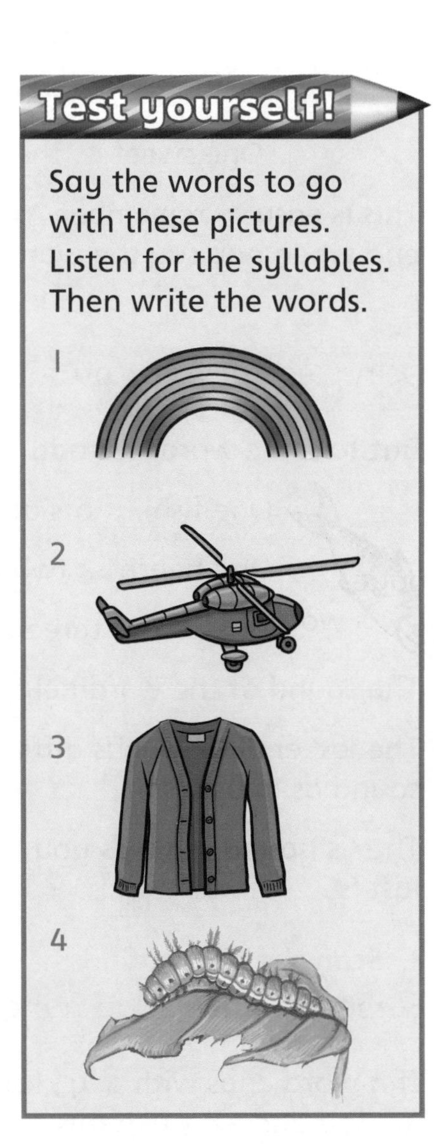

Remember

Break a long word into **syllables**. Then write the word one syllable at a time.

Breaking a word into syllables can also help you to read long words.

More than one?

Here is something to remember when spelling words. If there is more than one of something, we often put 's' on the end of the word. This makes it **plural**.

Adding 's' to make the plural

One star ... lots of star<u>s</u>

One dog ... two dog<u>s</u>

One sweet ... three sweet<u>s</u>

This is easy to remember. You can hear the 's' on the end when you say the words.

Using 'es' for other plurals

But to some words we add 'es', like this:

One fish ... lots of fish<u>es</u>

One bench ... two bench<u>es</u>

One box ... three box<u>es</u>

The sound of the word helps you remember this.

The 'es' ending sounds different. It makes an 'is' sound as in box<u>es</u>.

The 'is' sound reminds you to put 'es' on the end, not just 's'.

Something special to remember

If a word ends with a 'y', sometimes we take off the 'y' and add 'ies', like this:

One bab<u>y</u> ... two bab<u>ies</u>

Look out for other words like this!

Test yourself!

Write the words to go with these pictures.

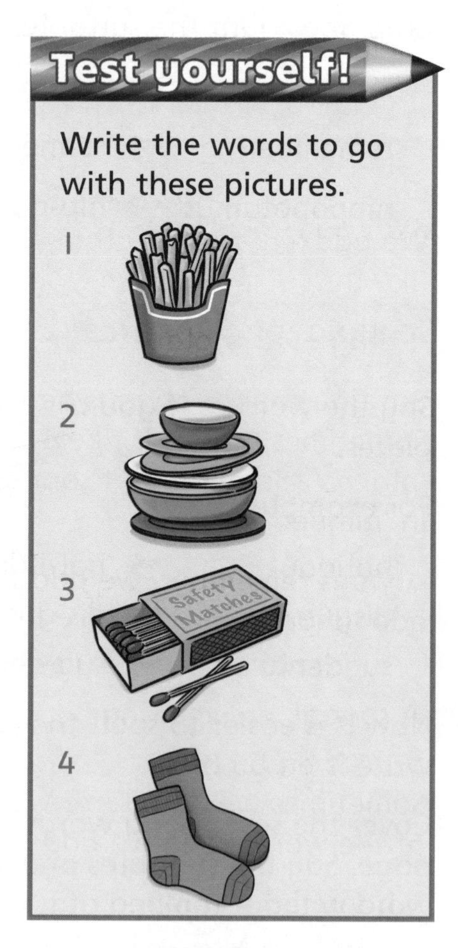

Remember

Listen for **plural endings**. Add an **'s'** to the end of most words. But if the word ends with an 'is' sound, add **'es'**.

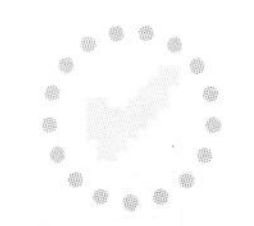

Word endings 'ing' and 'ed'

Some words say what people are doing. These words are called verbs. We often put 'ing' or 'ed' on the end of verbs.

Adding 'ing'

We add 'ing' to show something is happening. You write the word and then put 'ing' on the end, like this:

play + ing = playing   jump + ing = jumping

But if a word ends with an 'e', you leave off the 'e' when you add 'ing':

hid$_e$ + ing = hiding   slid$_e$ + ing = sliding

Adding 'ed'

We add 'ed' to show that something has happened, like this:

play + ed = played   jump + ed = jumped

But you cannot always hear the 'ed' clearly. Sometimes it sounds like a 'd' on the end, as in 'played'. Sometimes it sounds like a 't' on the end, as in 'jumped'.

Always remember, we add 'ed' to verbs. We do **not** add 'd' or 't'.

A special 'ed' spelling

Sometimes we double the last letter of the word when we add 'ed':

hop + ed = hopped

stop + ed = stopped

Test yourself!

Add 'ing' to these words

1 a) throw
b) smile
c) pull
d) come

2 Add 'ed' to these words:
a) show
b) ask
c) shout
d) clap

Remember

You will often need to add **'ing'** and **'ed'** to the end of verbs.

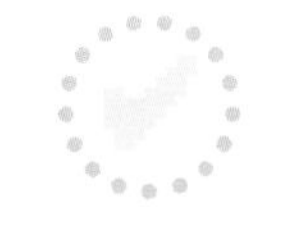

Learning to spell tricky words

You cannot spell all words just by breaking them down into **phonemes**. Some words have tricky bits that are not spelt as they sound – words like:

said you sure

You can learn to spell tricky words. Just follow these steps.

1

First you **look** at the word.

2

Then you **say** it. Can you spot the tricky bit? Underline the tricky bit to help you remember it.

said

3

Now **cover** the word.

4

Try to **write** it while it is still covered up. Think carefully about the tricky bit!

5

Finally, **check** your spelling to see if you are right.

Remember, you can always use a **dictionary** to check your spelling.

Test yourself!

Choose five tricky words you want to learn to spell. Check their correct spelling in a dictionary, or ask an adult. Use the ideas on this page to help you learn them.

Word families

Sometimes learning to spell one word can help you to spell other words.

Learn to spell the word 'the'. It helps you to spell all these words:

they then there these

You see, all these words start with the word 'the'!

Remember

Look and **say** a word to find the tricky bit. **Cover** the word and **write** it. **Check** you have spelt it right. **Look–say–cover–write–check**!

Checking what you have learned

First, check that you can **read** all the words on this page. Then use the ideas on page 52 to help you learn how to **spell** them.

Tricky words

are	good	little	old	saw	was
because	have	more	people	school	were
boy	house	new	said	want	you
do	laugh				

Word families

Some words that sound similar are in the same **word family**. They are spelt in a similar way. Knowing a word family will help you to spell the words within it.

the – they – then – there – these

that – this – than

what – when – who – why – which

other – another – brother – mother

an – any – many

our – your – four

here – there – where

all – call – ball

out – about – shout

after – sister – water

could – should – would

look – took – book

come – some

one – once

Test yourself!

Ask an adult to test you to see if you can spell all the words in the two boxes above. Ask the adult to say the words and see if you can write them down.

Handwriting

Your handwriting is important because you want people to read what you have written. If writing is untidy, no-one can read it.

Here are some important things to remember about handwriting.

- Always leave **spaces between words**.

  Itishardtoreadwritingwithnospaces ✗

  (That says: *It is hard to read writing with no spaces!*)

- Do not mix up capital letters and lower case letters. Do not put a capital letter in the middle of a word.

  woRds ✗

- Make sure all your letters are the **right shape** and the **right way round**, like this:

  c o a d g q
  l b h k t
  r n m p
  i u w y j
  v x z
  e s f

- Remember that some letters need **sticks** ('ascenders') and some letters need **tails** ('descenders').

  Letters with sticks: b d f h k l t

  Letters with tails: f g j p q y

Test yourself!

Write out this rhyme in your best handwriting.

Star light, star bright
First star I see tonight.
I wish I may, I wish I might
Have the wish I wish tonight.

Remember

Write clearly. Make sure that all your letters are the right shape and size.

Answers

For some questions there is more than one correct answer. If you are not sure whether your answer is right, ask an adult to help you.

Page 4

1 "Hello, <u>like</u> (little) girl," said the big bad wolf. (The underlined word should be 'little'.)

2 The frog <u>helped</u> (hopped) off into the pond. (The underlined word should be 'hopped'.)

3 We all went on a <u>trap</u> (trip) to the zoo. (The underlined word should be 'trip'.)

Pages 6–7

Here are some examples of words or names you might have found:

Consonant phonemes:

1 a) chop, b) shop, c) thin, d) duck

Long vowel phonemes:

1 a) see, b) dream, c) evening
2 a) paint, b) day, c) name
3 a) lie, b) bite, c) night, d) sky
4 a) road, b) show, c) pole, d) Joe
5 a) room, b) glue, c) rule, d) new
6 a) storm, b) floor, c) straw, d) more
7 a) sir, b) burn, c) term, d) search
8 a) boy, b) soil
9 a) down, b) out
10 a) far
11 a) fair, b) wear, c) share
12 a) year, b) beer, c) here

Page 10

1 one spring morning
2 he dived around trying to catch fish
3 under a tree
4 Oscar had no fish
5 he ate fish

Page 11

1 because he had tricked Oscar **or** because it was what he wanted Oscar to say
2 because he wanted Oscar to think he was getting tired
3 because he thought there would be more fish the next day
4 because he had done all the fishing the day before

Page 12

1 No, because Oscar was not very clever to fall for his brother's tricks.
2 Here you can answer 'Yes' **or** 'No'. But the reason you give must come from the story. For example: 'No, because he tricked his brother into doing all the work and took all the fish.' **or** 'Yes, because his brother was lazy and wanted him to do all the work.'
3 You can answer this question with 'Yes' **or** 'No' as long as you give a reason that mentions something in the story.

Page 13

1 he was a fruit seller
2 he was kind and helpful because he helped to carry the old man's heavy load
3 because he cannot climb up to get the best fruit to sell

Page 14

1 a recipe and a letter
2 a dictionary

Page 15

1 to make each ingredient stand out, so it is easy to check
2 to help readers quickly find the word they want
3 so you can glance at the page and find out what it is about

Answers

Page 16

1 caterpillars are the young of butterflies

2 so that they grow bigger

3 when they are fully grown

Page 17

1 tiny scales, which look like dust

2 with its long tongue

3 nectar from flowers

4 how big they are compared to wasps and ladybirds **or** that they are 4–5 cm long **or** that they are longer than wasps and ladybirds

Page 19

1 a) metal, glass, paper
   b) Any three of the following: put paper (newspapers), cans and bottles in a recycling box; take things to a charity shop; put vegetable peelings in a compost bin; use plastic bags again

2 a) because getting rid of rubbish is bad for the environment **or** because if we do not recycle we throw away useful materials
   b) because it says many people now use recycling boxes or recycling points
   c) You can choose anything mentioned in the text, but you must (in 'd') give a reason for your choice. For example:
      Re-use carrier bags
   d) because otherwise we use about 10 new ones every week.

Page 20

1 snail and trail

2 any three from: busy, bee, buzzing, by, buzzily

3 It is on a line by itself. It is written with lots of 'z's.

Page 21

1 fields, trees, umbrellas, ships at sea

2 that it rains in lots of different places

Page 22

Make sure each sentence makes sense and gives one piece of information.
Make sure you have put three capital letters and three full stops.

Here is an example:

My favourite game is football. You need two teams to play the game. There are 11 players in each team.

Page 23

Make sure each sentence makes sense. Make sure you have put a full stop at the end of each sentence. Here are some examples:

1 It was hot **so** we opened the window.

2 Jack ran away **but** the giant ran after him.

3 The phone rang **and** Mum went to answer it.

Page 24

Make sure each sentence makes sense. Make sure you have put a full stop at the end of the complete sentence.

Here are some examples of how you might have finished the sentences:

1 A dictionary is very useful because it helps you spell words.

2 Joe was in a hurry because he was late.

3 The ice started to melt because it was so hot.

4 Ben was happy when he won the race.

5 We went to bed when it was dark.

Page 25

Here are some examples:

1 On Saturday afternoon, Dan rode his bike in the park.

2 During the night, Carrie quietly slipped out of the door.

3 The dog ran madly round the garden.

Answers

Page 26
Here are some examples of more colourful sentences:

1 The little old lady was proudly wearing an enormous straw hat.
2 The big bad wolf quickly climbed the tallest tree.
3 Huge waves crashed noisily onto the dark rocks.

Page 28
1 Something like: we had our faces painted
2 Something like: insects, squirrels

Page 29
Here are some examples:

1 It was really breezy and everything kept blowing over. We even had sand in the sandwiches!
2 It has six legs. Ants live in a nest under the ground.

Page 30
1 chatty, informal, friendly
2 formal and polite
3 bossy

Page 31
1 Flakes of snow began to fall.
2 Fill the flowerpot with compost (or soil).
3 The lolly stick floated on the water.

Page 32
Check out your letter:

- Have you put the address and date at the top?
- Have you started the letter: 'Dear Baby Bear'?
- Have you told Baby Bear all about the party?
- Have you put in some interesting bits?
- Does your letter sound friendly and chatty?
- Have you ended your letter: 'from Goldilocks'?

Page 33
Check out your recount:

- Does the first sentence say what special event you are writing about?
- Have you written about the events in order?
- Have you used linking words like: 'First', 'Next', 'After that'?
- Have you put in some interesting details?
- Does your recount have an ending?

Page 34
Here is an example of what you might have written:

We built a huge sandcastle and put a flag on top. Then we watched the waves slowly flatten it!

Page 35
Here is an example of what you might have written about birds:

Birds are animals with feathers. They have wings and can fly. There are lots of different sorts of birds, for example, blackbirds, sparrows and thrushes. Lots of birds build nests in trees and bushes but some live in nest boxes or in the roofs of buildings.

Page 36
Check out your instructions:

- Have you put a heading (e.g. 'How to grow a giant sunflower')?
- Have you made a list of things needed?
- Did you break the instructions into steps?
- Did you use numbers or bullet points?
- Do your instructions tell the reader what to do (e.g., 'Water the seeds every day.')?
- Do your instructions go right to the end (e.g. 'In a few weeks you will have a lovely giant sunflower')?

Answers

Page 37

Here are some examples of ideas:

- Characters: a genie or a fairy; a poor boy or a lonely little girl
- Setting: a wood, a little cottage or a castle
- Events: finding a magic object, making a wish, becoming rich

Page 38

Make sure your plan has a beginning, a middle and an end.

Page 39

Here are some examples:

1 All of a sudden there was a puff of smoke.

2 Eventually he reached the top of the beanstalk.

3 The next morning they woke up cold and hungry.

Page 40

Here is an example of how you might have made it more interesting:

Suddenly there was a splash. Harry looked up in surprise and stared into the breaking waves. There was something there. It was glinting in the sunlight. It seemed to be made of glass.

Page 41

Here are some examples of words you might have chosen:

1 The little mouse peered/peeked round the corner.

2 The cake was delicious/yummy/scrumptious.

3 "Please let me go!" begged/pleaded/sobbed the tiny alien.

Page 42

1 It was 12 o'clock. Cinderella ran out of the palace.

2 The monster was close by. Alex listened for his footsteps.

Page 43

- Check that your poem uses interesting words.
- Check that each new line starts with a capital letter.
- Check that the poem sounds like a poem (e.g. it might use rhyme or words that start with the same letter).

Page 44

We went into the playground. On the grass there was a climbing frame with a rope ladder. Next to it was a sand pit.

Page 45

1 That is amazing!

2 What time is it?

3 Can I help you?

4 Help, save me!

Page 46

1 "Stop!" shouted the policeman.

2 I had pizza, salad and ice cream for tea.

3 "I can help you", said the boy.

4 We play rounders, cricket, netball and football.

Page 47

1 milk

2 brush

3 clock

4 belt

Page 48

1 fork

2 gate

3 light

4 bowl

Page 49

1 rainbow

2 helicopter

3 cardigan

4 caterpillar

Answers

Page 50

1 chips

2 dishes

3 matches

4 socks

Page 51

1 a) throwing
  b) smiling
  c) pulling
  d) coming

2 a) showed
  b) asked
  c) shouted
  d) clapped

Page 52

Learn the spellings using the five steps: look–say–cover–write–check. You can also use word families to help you (see page 53).

Page 53

Check your spellings against the words listed on page 53.

Page 54

Ask an adult to help you to check your handwriting.

Curriculum chart

Primary Framework for literacy: Reading objectives

(Year 2 unless otherwise indicated)

Word recognition: decoding (reading) and encoding (spelling)	Revision Guide topics	pages
Recognise and use alternative ways of pronouncing the graphemes already taught (Y1)	Blending phonemes, Blending more phonemes	6, 7
Recognise and use alternative ways of spelling the phonemes already taught, for example that the /ae/ sound can be spelt with 'ai', 'ay' or 'a-e' (Y1)	Blending phonemes, Blending more phonemes	6, 7
Identify the constituent parts of two-syllable and three-syllable words to support the application of phonic knowledge and skills (Y1)	Reading difficult words, Using syllables to help with spelling	5, 49
Read and spell phonically decodable two-syllable and three-syllable words (Y1)	Reading difficult words, Using syllables to help with spelling	5, 49
Read independently and with increasing fluency longer and less familiar texts	Reading for meaning, Reading a story, Reading a non-fiction text	4, 8, 14
Know how to tackle unfamiliar words that are not completely decodable	Reading difficult words	5
Read and spell less common alternative graphemes including trigraphs	Blending phonemes, Blending more phonemes	6, 7
Read high and medium frequency words independently and automatically	Checking what you have learned	53

Word structure and spelling		
Segment sounds into their constituent phonemes in order to spell them correctly. Children move from spelling simple CVC words to longer words that include common digraphs and adjacent consonants such as 'brush', 'crunch' (Y1)	Breaking words down	47
Recognise and use alternative ways of spelling the graphemes already taught, for example that the /ae/ sound can be spelt with 'ai', 'ay' or 'a-e'... (Y1)	Blending phonemes, Blending more phonemes, Words with long vowel sounds	6, 7, 48
Use knowledge of common inflections in spelling, such as plurals ... (Y1)	More than one?	50
Read and spell phonically decodable two-syllable and three-syllable words (Y1)	Using syllables to help with spelling	49
Spell with increasing accuracy and confidence, drawing on word recognition and knowledge of word structure, and spelling patterns including common inflections and use of double letters	Word endings 'ing' and 'ed', Learning to spell tricky words, Checking what you have learned	51, 52, 53
Read and spell less common alternative graphemes including trigraphs	Blending phonemes, Blending more phonemes	6, 7

Understanding and interpreting texts		
Identify the main events and characters in stories and find specific information in simple texts (Y1)	Checking your understanding, Finding answers	10, 16
Explore the effect of patterns of language and repeated words and phrases (Y1)	Reading a poem	20
Draw together ideas and information from across a whole text, using simple signposts in the text	Thinking about the facts, Features of non-fiction texts	19, 15
Give some reasons why things happen or characters change	Explaining why, Thinking about characters	11, 13
Explain organisational features of texts, including alphabetical order, layout, diagrams, captions	Features of non-fiction texts, Information in pictures	15, 17
Explore how particular words are used, including words and expressions with similar meanings	Thinking about a poem, Finding the best word	21, 41

continued opposite

Curriculum chart

Engaging with and responding to texts	Revision Guide topics	pages
Visualise and comment on events, characters and ideas (Y1)	Reading a story	8
Distinguish fiction and non-fiction texts and the different purposes for reading them (Y1)	Reading a non-fiction text	14
Explain their reactions to texts, commenting on important aspects	What do you think? Thinking about the facts	12, 19

Primary Framework for literacy: Writing objectives

(Year 2 unless otherwise indicated)

Creating and shaping texts	Revision Guide topics	pages
Use key features of narrative in their own writing (Y1)	Thinking of ideas	37
Convey information and ideas in simple non-narrative forms (Y1)	Adding detail	29
Draw on knowledge and experience of texts in deciding and planning what and how to write	Types of non-fiction writing, The right word, Writing a letter, Writing a recount, Writing a postcard and writing a diary, Writing a report, Writing instructions, Thinking of ideas	27, 31, 32–36, 37
Sustain form in narrative, including use of person and time	The details of the story, Checking your writing	40, 42
Maintain consistency in non-narrative, including purpose and tense	How does it sound?	30
Make adventurous word and language choices appropriate to the style and purpose of the text	The right word, Finding the best word	31, 41
Select from different presentational features to suit particular writing purposes	Writing a letter, Writing a recount, Writing a postcard and writing a diary, Writing a report, Writing instructions	32–36

Text structure and organisation	Revision Guide topics	pages
Group written sentences together in chunks of meaning or subject (Y1)	Adding detail	29
Use planning to establish clear sections for writing	Stop, think and organise! Planning the story	28, 38
Use appropriate language to make sections hang together	Using time links	39

Sentence structure and punctuation	Revision Guide topics	pages
Compose and write simple sentences independently to communicate meaning (Y1)	Writing in sentences	22
Use capital letters and full stops when punctuating simple sentences (Y1)	Full stops and capital letters	44
Write simple and compound sentences and begin to use subordination in relation to time and reason	Linking ideas together, More linking words	23, 24
Compose sentences using tense consistently	Checking your writing	42
Use question marks, and use commas to separate items in a list	Question marks and exclamation marks, Commas and speech marks	45, 46
Compose sentences using adjectives, verbs and nouns for precision, clarity and impact (Y3)	Interesting sentences, Colourful sentences	25, 26

Presentation	Revision Guide topics	pages
Write most letters, correctly formed and orientated, using a comfortable and efficient pencil grip (Y1)	Handwriting	54
Write legibly, using upper and lower case letters appropriately within words, and observing correct spacing within and between words	Handwriting	54

Glossary

alphabetical order	words put into order using the first letter of each word (e.g. in an index). Words starting with 'a' go before words starting with 'b', etc.
blending	putting sounds together to make a word (e.g. the sounds 'c-a-t' blend to make 'cat')
bullet points	a list of short points on separate lines – each point is marked with a big dot or symbol
capital	a special way of writing each letter (e.g. 'A', 'B'). Capital letters are used at special times, as at the start of a sentence or a name. They are also called upper case letters
character	someone in a story. A character can be a person or an animal
chart	facts arranged in a diagram or table
comma	looks like this , and is used to show a little break in a sentence
consonant	any of the letters in the alphabet that is not a vowel (e.g. b, c, d, f, g)
contents	a list showing what is on each page of a book. It is found at the front of a book
description	words that create for the reader a picture of a person, place or object
diary	a daily note of events
dictionary	a book that lists lots of words in alphabetical order and is used to check spelling; it might also give the meaning of the words
events	things that happen
exclamation mark	looks like this ! and is used at the end of an exclamation (e.g. "What a noise!")
facts	pieces of true information
fiction	something that has been made up and is not based on facts
flowchart	a diagram that shows a series of events
full stop	looks like this . and is used at the end of a sentence
headings	titles that say what the text is about. Headings are usually in bigger or bolder print than the rest of the page
index	a list of subjects found in a book put into alphabetical order; the page number is next to each subject
information	facts or news about something
key words	the most important words in a sentence, question or piece of text
language	written or spoken words
lower case	lower-case letters (e.g. 'a', 'b', 'c') are not capital letters
non-fiction	writing that is based on fact and is not made up
notes	a few key words used as a reminder. A note is not written as a full sentence
past tense	the verbs you use when something has already happened (e.g. "We went to the park." or "I won a PlayStation.")
phonemes	the sounds in a word (e.g. the word 'dog' has three phonemes: 'd-o-g')

Glossary

plural	more than one of something (e.g. 'dogs')
poet	the person who writes a poem
punctuation	written marks like full stops, question marks and exclamation marks
question mark	looks like this ? and is used at the end of a question
recipe	instructions for how to prepare food or cook something
rhyme	words that have the same sound at the end (e.g. bin, tin).
rhythm	the beat of the words in a poem
scan	look quickly over a text looking for a particular word
segmenting	breaking down a word into its separate phonemes (sounds) (e.g. you can segment the word 'sad' into 's-a-d')
sentence	words are put together to make a sentence
setting	the place where a story takes place
skim	look quickly over some text to get an idea of what it is about
speech marks	look like this " " and are used to show when someone is speaking
story	a fiction text, usually about made-up characters and events
storyboard	a series of boxes showing the main events in a story
sub-heading	a heading that is not the main heading at the top of the page. It says what a section of text is about
syllable	small parts of a word. Each syllable makes a separate sound or beat when you say the word (e.g. 'gar-den' has two syllables)
table	facts or numbers neatly arranged in lines
text	anything that is written or typed
upper case	another name for capital letters
verbs	'doing' words like 'catch', 'throw', 'run', 'jump'
vowel	any one of the letters 'a', 'e', 'i', 'o', or 'u'

Index

alphabetical order **15**

because **11, 24, 25**
blend **5, 6, 7**
bullet points **15**

capital letters **22, 43, 44, 54**
caption **17**
character **8, 13, 37, 40, 42, 46**
comma **46**
consonant **6**
contents page **15**

describe **26, 29, 40, 41**
diagram **17, 36**
diary **34**
dictionary **14**

events **8, 12, 26, 28, 33, 37, 38, 39, 40, 42**
exclamation mark **45**
explain **11, 12, 24**

flowchart **28**
full stop **22, 23, 39, 44**

handwriting **54**
heading **15, 35, 36**

index **15**
instructions **27, 30, 36**
invitation **30**

key words **14, 16**

labels **17**
letter **14, 27, 30, 32, 34**
linking words **23, 24, 33, 39**
list **15, 36, 46**
lower case **54**

notes **38**

order **8, 15, 28, 33, 36, 38, 39**
organise **28, 35**

past tense **42**
phoneme **6, 7, 47, 48**
planning **28, 38**
plural **50**
poem **20, 21, 43**
poet **20, 21**
postcard **27, 30, 34**

question mark **45**

reasons **11, 12, 19, 24**
recipe **14, 31, 36**
recount **33, 34**
report **27, 35**
rhyme **20, 43**
rhythm **20**

scanning **14, 16**
segmenting **47**
sentence **22, 23, 24, 25, 26, 29, 39, 44, 45, 46**
setting **37, 40**
skimming **14**
sound pattern **20, 43**
speech marks **46**
storyboard **38**
story language **37, 40**
sub-heading **15, 35**
syllable **5, 49**

text box **15**

upper case **63**

verbs **51**
vowel **6, 7, 48**

'why' questions **11, 19**